Grace Paley

New and Collected Poems

Tilbury House, Publishers
Gardiner, Maine

Tilbury House, Publishers
132 Water Street
Gardiner, ME 04345

First Printing, January, 1992.

Library of Congress Cataloging-in-Publication Data

Paley, Grace.
    [Poems. Selections]
    New and collected poems / Grace Paley.
        p.   cm.
    ISBN 0-88448-098-4 : $19.95. -- ISBN 0-88448-099-2 (pbk.) : $12.95
    I. Title
PS3566.A46A6   1992
811'.54--dc20   91-44787
                                                                    CIP

Acknowledgements

Some of the poems in this collection were first published, some in slightly different versions, in the following books:
Leaning Forward, Granite Press, 1985;
365 Reasons Not to Have Another War, War Resisters League, 1989;
Long Walks and Intimate Talks, The Feminist Press, 1991;

and magazines:
Chelsea, Field, Ikon, Persea, Shankpainter, Sunbury, Win Magazine, Alaska Quarterly Review, Women and Art.

"What would happen" was issued as a broadside in a letterpress limited edition under the title, "Goldenrod," Granite Press, 1983, Penobscot, Maine.

"Families" and "On the Ramblas   A Tree   A Girl" are reprinted by permission of The Feminist Press at the City University of New York from *Long Walks and Intimate Talks* by Grace Paley, 1991.

The publisher and author would like to extend special thanks to Bea Gates for extracting many of the poems in this book from Grace Paley's notebooks.

And special thanks to Jane Cooper.

Contents

for Bob

Grace Paley

New and Collected Poems

I

A woman invented fire and called it
                    the wheel
Was it because the sun is round
          I saw the round sun bleeding to sky
And fire rolls across the field
          from forest to treetop
It leaps like a bike with a wild boy riding it

oh   she said
          see the orange wheel of heat
light that took me from the
          window of my mother's home
to home in the evening

3

Stanzas: Old Age and the Conventions of Retirement
Have Driven My Friends from the Work They Love

1

When she was young she wanted
to sing in a bank
a song about money
            the lyrics of gold
was her song
            she dressed for it

2

She did good. She stood up like a
planted flower among yellow weeds
            turning to please the sun
            they were all shiny
it was known she was planted

3

No metaphor reinvents the job of the nurture of children
except to muddy or mock.

4

the job of hunting of shooting in hunting season of
standing alone in the woods of being an Indian

4

5

The municipal center
the morning of anger
the centrifugal dream
her voice flung out on plates of rage
       then they were put in a paper sack
       she was sent to the china closet
       and never came back

6

Every day he went out, forsaking
wife and child
with his black bag he accompanied
the needle of pain as it
sewed our lives to death

7

One day at work   he cried
I am in my full powers
       suddenly he was blind
when slabs of time and aperture returned
dear friend   we asked
       what do you see
he said   I only see what has been
       seen already

One day when I was a child   long ago
Mr. Long Ago spoke up in school
He said
Oh children you must roll your r's
no no not on your tongue little girl
IN YOUR THROAT
there is nothing so beautiful as r rolled in the throat of a French woman
no woman more beautiful
he said   looking back
                  back
                  at beauty

Drowning (I)

If I were in the middle of the Atlantic
        drowning   far from home
I would look up at the sky
        veil of my hiding life
and say:
        goodbye

then I would sink

the second time I'd come up   I'd say:
                these are the willful waves of the watery sea
                which is drowning me
then I would sink
the third time I'd come up: it would be my last
                my arms   reaching
                my knees   falling
I'd cry   oh   oh
                first friend of my thinking head
                dear flesh
                farewell

Drowning (II)

This is how come I am drowned:
    First the sun shone on me
    Then the wind blew over me
    Then the sand polished me
    Then the sea touched me
    Then the tide came

Life

Some people set themselves tasks
other people say   do anything   only live
still others say
            oh oh   I will never forget you   event of my first life

The women let the tide go out
                    which will return   which will return
the sand, the salt, the fat drowned babies
The men ran furiously
                    along the banks of the estuary
screaming
          Come back you fucking sea
right now
          right now

A Poem About Storytelling

The artist comes next
she tells the story of the stories

The first person may be the child who
says   Listen!   Guess what happened!
The important listener is the mother
The mother says   What?

The first person can be the neighbor
She says   Today my son told me   Goodbye
I said   Really?   Who are you?   You
didn't even say hello yet   The listener
is probably her friend   She remembers
Well wasn't he always like that   as a small boy
I mean   The neighbor says   That's not
true   You're absolutely wrong   He was like a
motorcycle   a little horse   every now
and then at rest   a flower

The first person is often the lover who
says I never knew anyone like you
The listener is the beloved   She whispers
Who?   Me?

The first person is the giver of testimony
He rises and tells   I lived in that village
My father shouted   He returned from the fields
I was too small   My father cried out
Why don't you grow up and help me   my mother said
Help him   you're eight years old   it's time
The listeners say   Oh!   it was just
like that   I remember

11

The giver of testimony rises and tells
I lived in the hut   behind the barn
The padron   the manager   the master came
to me   I can take you whenever I want
he said   Now you're old enough   The right
age is twelve he said   The giver of testimony
rises   She looks into her village   she
looks into the next village   Where
are the listeners

The artist comes next   She waits for
the listeners too   What if they're all dead or
deafened by grief or in prison   Then
there's   no way out of it   She will listen
It's her work   She will be the listener
in the story of the stories

A Warning

One day I forgot Jerusalem and my right arm is withered
My right arm, my moving arm, my rising and falling arm
                        my loving arm
Is withered

And my left eye, the blinker and winker is plucked out
It hangs by six threads of endless remembering.
Because I forgot Jerusalem
And wherever I go, I am known, I am recognized at once. I am
                        perceived by strangers.
Because on one day, only one day I forgot Jerusalem.

Jews everywhere, Jews, old deaths of the north and south
                        kingdoms,
Poor Jews in the ghetto walls built by the noble slav,
                        Jew princes
In Amsterdam who live in diamond houses that shine like window
                        panes
Listen to me. Wherever you go, keep the nation of that city
                        in mind
For I forgot her and now I am blind and crippled.

Even my lover, a Christian with pale eyes and the barbarian's foreskin
                        has left me.

The veins that stand on the back of my sunburned hand
are something like the branched veins on the flat tan
                    shore of the bay
Out of these, when the tide tugs
salt sea runs   back
into the rocky basin from which
we came
on the first day   specks
in a stranded pool   dashed
in high tide   alive
on the hot dry land.

At the Battery

I am standing on one foot
at the prow of great Manhattan
leaning forward
projecting a little into the bright harbor

If only a topographer in a helicopter
would pass over my shadow
I might be imposed forever
on the maps of this city

An Arboreal Mystery

On Jane Street in October
I saw three gingko trees
    the first is naked to the bony branch
    the second is a dance of little golden fans
    the third is green as green September

20th Street   Spring

the wives of the black-sailed seminarians
take their children to walk with green pails

they are light-haired and slim   their husbands are studying
passion and service   the seminary

is old the baby leaves of the old sycamores are pale green
are river yellow   like the high light arms of the sycamore

the seminary is red and soot-darkened
by the soot-making city   it is at the side of the city near the river

it stands aside from the piers and the warehouses and the longshoremen
it intends to be quiet and dark   though sunlight surrounds it

sun lies on the streets and the lawns and the children
of the seminarians play with red hoops in the street in the sun

note to grandparents

the children are healthy
    the children are rosy
we take them to the park
    we take them to the playground

they swing on the swings
    the wind smacks their faces
they jump and are lively
    they eat everything

they sleep without crying
    they are very smart
each day they grow
    you would hardly know them

psalm

their shoes are stuccoed with sawdust and blood
the two young butchers walk singing together on ninth avenue
the sun is out because it is the lunch hour
they kick the melting snow and splash into deep puddles
then they embrace one another in the cold air
for water and singing may wash away the blood of the lamb

Mulberry Street ends in good works
The Committee for Nonviolent Action begins there
Also St. Barnabas House which shelters abandoned children

And on the corner of Mott Street
Bob Nichols is making a playground
single-handed   two mountains   an iron tower from which
the cliffs of Houston Street can be observed
a maple glade   a ship at sea

The boys from St. Bernard's
and the boys from
Our Lady of Pompeii
converge on the corner of Bleecker and Bank

There is a grinding of snowballs
and a creaking of ice

The name of our Lord is invoked

But for such healthy tough warriors
He has other deaths in mind

Sulky
They part

For Danny

My son enters the classroom
There are thirty two children waiting for him
He dreams that he will teach them to read
His head is full of the letters that words are looking for

Because of his nature
his fingers are flowers
Here is a rose   he says   look   it grew right
into the letter R

They like that idea very much   they lean forward
So he says   now spell garden
They write it correctly in their notebooks   maybe
          because the word rose is in it

My son is happy
Now spell sky
For this simple word the children
turn their eyes down and away   doesn't he know
the city has been quarreling with the sky all of their lives

Well, he says spell   home   he's a little frightened
          to ask this of them   What?
They laugh   they can't hear him say
What's so funny?   they jump
up out of their seats laughing

My son says hopefully   it's three o'clock
but they don't want to leave   where will they go?
they want to stay right here in the classroom   they probably
want to spell garden again   they want
to examine his hand

The Nature of This City

Children walking with their grandmothers
talk foreign languages
that is the nature of this city
and also this country

Talk is cheap but comes in variety
and witnessing dialect
there is a rule for all
and in each sentence a perfect grammar

On the Fourth Floor

The woman on the fourth floor said You slut! don't you knock on my
             door   stand up straight   be a woman!
The girl said   I ain't a slut   I didn't have no father   my mother. . .
The woman said   Stop that   neither did I   I didn't have nothin
The girl said   I ain't a slut   I don't fuck guys
The woman said   Who cares about guys   you're disgusting   you ain't
             a woman
You're dirty   look at you   you can't keep your eyes open

The boy came to the head of the stairs   He hollered   Diana come up
             here   where's the tuinals
The girl said I ain't got them
The boy screamed   I had sixteen   I ate ten   I give you four   there's
             two left someplace
I ain't got them   I only got two methodone
Look at you   the boy said   you hung down to the ground   you ate them
I didn't   she said come with me Eddie
to the East River Drive   There's a party   I'll say you're my husband
The boy screamed   get me the two tuinal

The woman took the girl's hand Go into your house   right this
             minute   pay him no mind
wash up   you stink   comb your hair   straight yourself
ain't you ashamed? Be a woman

Winter Afternoon

Old men and women walk by my window
they're frightened   it's icy wintertime
they take small steps   they're looking
at their feet   they're glad to be
going   they hate
the necessity

sometimes the women wear heels   why
do they do this   the old women's
heads are bent   they see   their shoes
which are often pointy   these shoes
were made for crossed legs in the
evening pointing

                        sometimes the old men
walk a dog   the dog moves too fast
the man stands still   the dog stands
still   the smells come to the dog
floating from the square earth of the
plane tree   from the tires of cars
at rest   all this interesting life
and adventure comes to the waiting dog
the man doesn't know this   the street
is too icy   old women in pointy shoes
and high heels pass him   their necks
in fur collars bent   their eyes watch
their small slippery feet

Middle Age Poem

                With what joy
I left home to deposit one thousand, one hundred and nineteen
            dollars in the bank
I was whistling and skipping
you would think I had a new baby and a new cradle
after so many years
or that my mother had come to visit from Queens, borough of
            cemeteries
you would think a lover
was waiting
at the corner of Chemical Trust
and First National
right under the willow oak
with open arms

Bob Visits Friends

Well I can see you   now
you are hurrying along the street
head down in order to not miss
any great event on the pavement
about to make a visit to somebody's life
Peter and Elka's   where the children
will   welcome you with bread and strawberries
they fly to a proper distance
nibbling rye crumbs by the healthy ton
sighing in Russian and singing in German

then you will extricate yourself
from the richness of kitchens and family
and cross town again because it's so early
the summer's first light hot hand
has made you feverish for encounter in air
at least by open window   so   now the sixth floor
overlooking Bedford Street   the open lot
that will not become the Broome Street Expressway

Because of this political victory and the birth
of a child there is a plan being made
in that small apartment
              TO BE GOOD AND HAPPY FOREVER
The fact is: this *can* be successful
if it starts late enough in life

On Mother's Day

I went out walking
in the old neighborhood

Look! more trees on the block
forget-me-nots all around them
ivy   lantana shining
and geraniums in the window

Twenty years ago
it was believed that the roots of trees
would insert themselves into gas lines
then fall   poisoned on houses and children

or tap the city's water pipes
or starved for nitrogen   obstruct the sewers

In those days in the afternoon I floated
by ferry to Hoboken or Staten Island
then pushed the babies in their carriages
along the river wall   observing Manhattan
See Manhattan I cried   New York!
even at sunset it doesn't shine
but stands in fire   charcoal to the waist

But this Sunday afternoon on Mother's Day
I walked west   and came to Hudson Street   tri-colored flags
were flying over old oak furniture for sale
brass bedsteads   copper pots and vases
by the pound from India

Suddenly before my eyes   twenty-two transvestites
in joyous parade stuffed pillows
under their lovely gowns

and entered a restaurant
under a sign which said   All Pregnant Mothers Free

I watched them place napkins over their bellies
and accept coffee and zabaglione

I am especially open to sadness and hilarity
since my father died as a child
one week ago in this his ninetieth year

Housing

Walking along a street in a neighborhood
where the black trashbags are stacked as neat
as a woodpile in Vermont   my lover said to me
oh will we ever live in a district like this
where the artists are growing old in brownstones
and their grandchildren visit them with watercolors
and pastels   if we could only find a
condominium or a coop like the one
on ninth street   where the tenants themselves
have lovingly laid a mulch of pine branches
among the roses

                then I answered my lover
It is probably too late for sentiment
of that kind   we are fated to create
our own community in the borough of
        Brooklyn   or Staten Island   though there are
many who are happy in the little cities
across the river in another state
where we might well establish patterns of
comfort and gently rising affluence
all of which requires of course that the earth
be not blown up or irremediably
poisoned and that you and I remain if not
lovers at least cordial creators of
family and continuity

Having Arrived by Bike at Battery Park

I thought I would
sit down at one of those park department tables
and write a poem honoring
the occasion which is May 25th
Evelyn   my best friend's birthday
and Willy Langbauer's birthday

Day! I love you for your delicacy
in appearing after so many years
as an afternoon in Battery Park right
on the curved water
where Manhattan was beached

At once arrows
straight as Broadway were driven
into the great Indian heart

Then we came from the east
seasick and safe the
white tormented people
grew fat in the
blood of that wound

II

A stranger calling a dog whistled
and I came running though I am not an afghan

or a highclass poodle and not much like a
city boy's dog with a happy wild tail and red eyes

The stranger said excuse me, I was calling my dog not you
Ah   I replied   to this courteous explanation

Sometimes I whistle too   but mostly for fear
of missing the world I am a dog to whistlers

For George (I)

What was left   before crumbling
was sweetness in the maple leaf

in our friend George   a brilliant
attentive sweetness

in the wild red maple leaf
before winter   in our friend
George Dennison   before death

For George (II)

The birds everywhere are talking
    about my friend George who is dying
What have the birds to do with it?
In their whistling songs they say   go south
    or else
George   they peck at his   window in Maine
    in the town of Temple
Go south   come with us   save yourself
    there's still time
But he refuses to leave   pain has trapped him
Pain keeps him at home

But if he had help?   If the children
whom he has after all immortalized in stories
    of their joyfulness with horses
If the children could help   if Mabel
    would help   if they stopped listening
to George's pain   if they saw the birds
how sure of themselves they are as they wrap up
    their northern affairs
and gather their swarming communities to   fly
float   sail   toward long sunlight
    south   south

on certain days I am not in love
and my heart turns over

       crowding the lungs for
       air

       driving blood in and out of
       the skull   improving my mind

       working muscles to the bone

       dashing resonance out of a roaring sea
       at my nerve endings

not much is needed

       air

       good sense

       power

       a noisy taking in and a
       loud giving back

then my heart like any properly turned
motor   takes off in sparks dragging all that machinery
through the blazing day
       like grass
           which our lord knows
           I am

One Day

One day   lying on my stomach in the afternoon   trying to sleep
I suffered penis envy (much to
                              my surprise

and with no belief in Freud   for years
                              in fact   extreme
antipathy)   what could I do but turn around

and close my eyes and dream of summer
                              in those days I
                              was a boy I whistled
at the gate for Tom

Then I woke up
then I slept
and dreamed another dream

in my drowned father's empty pocket
there were nine dollars and the salty sea
he said   I know you   my darling girl
you're the one that's me

The Five Day Week

The five-day week was set like a firecracker
The five-day week   ah   like a long bath in the
                first bathtub of God
The five-day week was sunny all year   (I remember)
The five-day week gave at last what she'd always longed for
                a cheerful noisy companion
                to Sabbath calm Queen of days

Some days I am lonesome   I want to talk to my mother
And she isn't home
Then I ask my father   Where has she been the last twenty years?
And he answers
Where do you think   you fool as usual?
      She is asleep in Abraham's bosom
      Resting from years of your incessant provocation
      Exhausted by infinite love of me
      Escaping from the boredom of days shortening to Christmas
          and the pain of days lengthening to Easter
      You know where she is   She is at ease in Zion with all
          the other dead Jews

I cannot keep my mind on Jerusalem
It wanders off like an idiot with no attention span
to whatever city lies outside my window that day
      Damascus
          the libraries of Babylonia
Oh! the five exogamous boroughs of
our beloved home New York

What will happen
when the Lord
remembers vengeance
(which is his)
and finds me

Family

My father was brilliant   embarrassed   funny   handsome
my mother was plain   serious   principled   kind
my grandmother was intelligent   lonesome for her
                    other life   her dead children   silent
my aunt was beautiful   bitter   angry   loving

I fell among these adjectives in earliest childhood
and was nearly buried with opportunity
some of them stuck to me   others
finding me American and smooth slipped away

Letter

I am writing to the
Chinese Association for the Study
of Jewish Literature

They have asked for the addresses
of a couple of other Jews
Ozick and Kazin to be specific

Of course there are hundreds
probably thousands now alive
writing in Spanish and Portuguese

Russian   even German   the great languages
of nations into whose histories
we were admitted and began almost

immediately to talk   exclaim   praise
make metaphor despair raise children
ask questions of the authorities

in their own tongue!   succeed multiply
and finally be driven out

They say   a thousand Jews fled Bombay
in the 12th century   travelled to
Kaifeng City to live in the center

of China   to live   to live   ah   into
the generations they disappeared
in the terrible Yahweh-defying act
of assimilation

My Mother: 33 Years Later

1

There are places
   garden
   music room
   stove
   dining room

death bed   her eyes are open   she doesn't speak
   my sister and I hold up a picture of Frannie the first grandchild
   Mama do you know who this is?
   Fools! Who do you think you're talking to?
   Oh! she cried and turned away

my room   she says
   I've heard that expression
   I know how you talk
   don't think I'm so dumb
   hot pants! that's what you say, you girls!

Bobby and I are walking, arm in arm, across the campfield
Our mothers are behind us. We're nine years old.
We're wearing swimming trunks.
                           She says
   look   see the line of soft soft
   hair along their spines
   like down   our little birds

One of the mothers
the mother out of whose body
I easily appeared

Once I remembered her

45

2

This is what I planned:
To get to the end of our life quickly

And begin again

Everyone is intact   talking
Mother and Father   Mira   Babashka
all of us eating our boiled egg
but the poplar tree on Hoe Avenue
has just been cut down and the Norway maple
is planted in Mahopac

Then
my mother gives me
a vase full of zinnias
"as straight as little Russian Soldiers"

yes
mama
as straight as the second grade
in the P.S. 50 school yard
at absolute attention
under its woolen hats
of pink   orange   lavender   yellow

On the Bank Street Pier

In the mind's eye
    the mind cries I I I
the mother's face
    the father's looking eye
then sees
    then says
the scrambled iron piers
    the river's broad as
    mother's face

In the mind's ear
    talk talk talk
    the tickling tongue
of strangers

Poets!
Madness is a gift
god-given
(though not to me)

the receiver
knows the secret exit
he need never
plan on death
the door open to all

sometimes
before my very eyes
I see him
slipping the lock
he winks
my gifted friend
he says   don't
take any wooden lovers
while I'm gone

lonesome
I bang on the door
of his locked kingdom

no love
      no love cried the last fling
            in the vase
            on the piano
no love
      her dress like a garden
            her knees
            in the water

her dress
      white peacocks with green tails

is that beautiful she said
                        beautiful he said
                        touching the marigold's dust

What has happened?
language eludes me
the nice   specifying
words of my life fail
when I call

Ah says a friend
dried up no doubt
on the dessicated
twigs in the swamp
of the skull like
a lake where the
waterlevel has been
shifted by highways
a couple of miles off

Another friend says
No no   My dear   perhaps
you are only meant to
speak more plainly

We quarreled
Alone I
turned away
from her dear
face then I
feared death

Question

Do you think old people should be put away
the one red rheumy eye   the pupil that goes back and back
the hands are scaly
                    do you think all that should be hidden

do you think young people should be seen so much on Saturday nights
hunting and singing in packs the way they do
standing on street corners looking this way and that

or the small children who are visible all the time everywhere
and have nothing to do but be smart
but be athletes
but jump
but climb high fences
                    do you think hearts should sink
                    do you think the arteries ought to crumble
                    when they could do good?
because the heart was made to endure
                    why does it not endure?
                    do you think this is the way it should be?

Old Age Porch

All morning they store suns
against the grave
         but this is useless
if you have ever seen a dead person
         you know it

Your friend lies in darkness   all
that sunlight spilled around her
in the   watery rays   you make a song
you invent the days
         of friendship

Fund Appeal

Against
    darkness
I send
    money
to the
    American
    Federation
    for the Blind

praying
    not so much
    to be spared
pain
    but for grap-
    pling nerve
    when I come

out of
    all arrival
    to the departure
    of senses.

For My Friend Who Planted a Tree for His Daughter Jane

Up here we don't plant trees   sometimes we take them down
we want to give back the cleared land   the farmers' hard work long ago

Because the forest moves easily on its red sumach and wild cherry toes
and near the pond the alder and willow stretch toward the tall reeds

They hold the swamp in place for a few years
then they lie down themselves and thicken the earth

So I have looked for a standing tree to call it
                                                    Jane

lovely child of my beloved friend   apple tree planted
one year ago I think you are Jane's tree

apple tree of earliest apples   apple tree of
the summer farmer who sees winter only once in awhile

In the cleared field you stand hemlock and pine
not too far off   and the birch tree   familiar

as the face of our Russian grandparents   white
as their friendly ghosts   I will say   Jane   in August

when the pale apples are ready   then we return
the core to earth   after frost the late apples

redden   grow tart with time and the cold nights   we look west
toward the valley villages   the small orchard   the fruit

early and late tumbled under light snow
sweet mulch of this sweet earth

Responsibility

It is the responsibility of society to let the poet be a poet
It is the responsibility of the poet to be a woman
It is the responsibility of the poet to stand on street corners
        giving out poems and beautifully written leaflets
        also leaflets they can hardly bear to look at
        because of the screaming rhetoric
It is the responsibility of the poet to be lazy to hang out and
        prophesy
It is the responsibility of the poet not to pay war taxes
It is the responsibility of the poet to go in and out of ivory
        towers and two-room apartments on Avenue C
        and buckwheat fields and army camps
It is the responsibility of the male poet to be a woman
It is the responsibility of the female poet to be a woman
It is the poet's responsibility to speak truth to power as the
        Quakers say
It is the poet's responsibility to learn the truth from the
        powerless
It is the responsibility of the poet to say many times: there is no
        freedom without justice and this means economic
        justice and love justice
It is the responsibility of the poet to sing this in all the original
        and traditional tunes of singing and telling poems
It is the responsibility of the poet to listen to gossip and pass it
        on in the way story tellers decant the story of life
There is no freedom without fear and bravery   there is no
        freedom unless
        earth and air and water continue and children
        also continue
It is the responsibility of the poet to be a woman   to keep an eye on
        this world and cry out like Cassandra, but be
        listened to this time.

III

Thetford Poems

Fear

I am afraid of nature
because of nature   I am mortal

my children and my grandchildren
are also mortal

I lived in the city for forty years
in this way   I escaped fear

Families

The sheep families are out in the meadow
Caddy and her two big lambs Gruff and Veronica
Veronica raises her curly head then bends to the grass
Usefully she shits   green grass and wool is her work

Gruff is going away   he will become something else
Father of generations? What?   more likely meat   that
is a male in war or pasture   his work is meat

What would happen
if there were a terrific shortage of goldenrod
in the world
and I put my foot outside this house
to walk in my garden and show city visitors
my two lovely rosebushes
and three remarkable goldenrod plants
that were doing well this year

I would say: Look!
how on each of several sprigs
there are two three dozen tiny stems
and on each stem three four tiny golden
flowers   petals stamen pistil and the pollen
which bees love
                    but insufficiently
otherwise
          can you imagine the fields
on rainy days in August   brass
streaking the lodged hayheads
dull brass in the rain
and under the hot sun
the golden flowers
               floating   gold dust of August fields
for miles and miles

what is this whiteness on the fields?
                    not rime
nor the Lord's snowy reason for exploding summer
it is the mist
                that starts the day
with drinks for all

When the wild strawberry leaves turn
red and show the dark place of the strawberries
it is too late

I know this has a
meaning inside my own life
inside dark life

Then Vera stopped at the flower called fireweed
three fireweed in that old field   year after year
I watch from the kitchen window and wonder why

when the earth is a repository of seed   a seed bank a
bed where seed rest comfortably   some say for years
waiting for the nudge from weather and light   year after

year   there are three fireweed   no more no less   then
Vera disappeared into the woods and our dog Bear
followed her   I said to myself   WORK! and walked

east toward the far sunny haze of Smartz mountain   down
into the swale   which had gathered vervain boneset and
meadowsweet   where were the beginnings of those late

asters that should have started their leaves towards
blue and lavender September   Still we are the gardeners
of this world and often talk about giving wildness

its chance   it's I who cut the field too late   too
early   right on time   and therefore out of the earth which
is a darkness of timed seed and waiting root the sunlight

chose vervain   jewel weed   boneset   just beyond
our woodchuck-argued garden a great nation of ants
has lived for fifteen years in a high sandy anthill

which   I honor with looking and looking and never disrupt
(nor have I learned their lesson of stubborn industry)
they ask nothing except to be not bothered and I personally

agree   though it is my nation that   has refined sugar
in jars of which   far from their sandy home   I've often
found them   drunk and bathing

In deepest summer
the milkweed flower
dries to pod in autumn
flies like seed and dies
in earth and is reborn

but not until
disaster strikes the field
and lays the grasses down
under the weighty ice
in which the water lives

St. Johnswort!
it must be summertime
buttercup   gone
hawkweed   gone

black eyed susan
          before you
know it   queen anne's lace

goldenrod and that
will be that

A bee!
drowning in
a wild rose
      flat on its
      round back
      kicking
too young to
use love for
health and
enrichment

An ant!
lugging half an ounce
of carcass across
the cement porch steps
       he's lost
       he struggled back and forth
       he carries a feast
       for his family
We can't find them
we looked under the steps
there wasn't a stray nation
anywhere

False strawberry is
an authentic five
petaled flower stand-

ing in a whirl of
three strawberry leaves
waiting in disturbed

fields for an accu-
mulation of the
healthy soil that kills

Then the flowers became very wild
because it was early September
and they had nothing to lose
they tossed their colors every
which way over the garden wall
splattering the lawn shoving their
wild orange red rain-disheveled faces
into my window without shame

I don't think
the rain will end
today   this is
because I come
from another
country

The Choir Singing

From the balcony of the Thetford Hill
First Congregational Church
I look down at the choir singing
the   adoration of Christ their Lord
the high foreheads of the older women
shine   why!   that's the very condition
of my own forehead which seemed in the
bathroom mirror to appear increasingly
intelligent this morning   the delicate
daily hair loss contributing   to the
reality and appearance of wisdom

Leaves   Apples

The golden maples had not yet begun their work
on behalf of beauty   the reds   like flowers
had sweetened to wine   bloody as house
geraniums   in a windy rage they were already
fallen   curled into dry claws   gone from themselves

and we were worn out with friends who'd traveled
three hundred miles because of their love of leaves
which they admired more than anything else
in nature   as for apples   they reminded us that
thousands were being piled at this very moment
into the fruit stalls of the Korean markets
of our old city

Connections: Vermont   Vietnam (I)

Hot summer day
on the River Road
swimmers of the Ompompanoosuc
dust in my eyes
          oh
          it is the hot wind from Laos
          the girl in Nhe An covers her face with a straw hat
          as we pass   she breathes   through cloth
          she stands between two piles of stone

          the dust of National Highway One blinds

me
summertime
I drive through Vermont
my fist on the horn, barefoot
          like Ching

Connections: Vermont   Vietnam (II)

The generals came to the president
We are the laughing stock of the world
What world? he said
                    the world
                    the world

Vermont
    the green world
    the green mountain

Across the valley
someone is clearing a field
he is making a tan rectangle
he has cut a tan rectangle on Lyme Hill
the dark wood
the deposed farm
                    the mist is sipped up by the sun
                    the mist is eaten by the sun

What world?   he said

What mountain?   said the 20 ships of the Seventh Fleet
rolling on the warm waves lobbing shells all the summer day
into green distance

        on Trung Son Mountain Phan Su told a joke:
        The mountain is torn, the trees are broken
        How easy it is to gather wood
        to repair my house in the village which is broken by bombs

His shirt is plum-colored, is brown like dark plums

the sails on the sampans that fish in the sea of the Seventh Fleet
                        are plum-colored

the holes in the mountain are red
the earth of that province is red   red
                                        world

IV

Song Stanzas of Private Luck

To Be Added To Sometimes
And Sometimes To Be Subtracted From
As Events Prove One More Wrong Than Right

Oh the year before I was born
        the sanitary napkin was invented
        the sanitary napkin
        the sanitary napkin
Nearly as important as the diaphragm
        more important
        for the girl child's first life
the cleanliness the sweetness
        the excellent   blood consuming
        sanitary napkin

(And in parenthesis   according
to the New York Times   in my 65th year
the women of Eritrea were freed
        to enter the legislature
        and the trenches
this was because a sanitary napkin factory
        had been established
        a state enterprise with
entrepreneurial intentions as remarkable as capitalism)

Oh the year I was born
        the Joint Distribution Committee
        the famous   now hardly known at all
        Joint Distribution Committee
travelled to Russia to save Jewish orphans
of which there were many
        though years later
        more   more   more
were made in another country and fewer were saved

Oh the year before I was born
        my mother and my father and
        my grandmother called Babashka
had already been in the U.S. for seventeen years
        and had missed civil war
        revolution and the terrible pogroms
        of Kishinev   Berditchev
they had been present for the pogrom of 1905   in which
our Rusya   our brother our uncle waving the workers' flag
        was murdered   the serious
        high-flying   bright red
        heavy   wind-enchanted
        workers flag

Oh but in the very year I was born
        our uncle Grisha was sent away
        was shipped away from home
        to die in his   own old country
brand new Russia   oh the year that I was born
        no one told me any of this
        none of the above was mentioned
the word deportation was not said
        the word anarchist
        the word Palmer raid
the year that I was born was never spoken of
as the year of exile   of life-long sorrow
that year was never mentioned to me
        by my father or my mother

except to say
ah   have we already   told you how
        we were longing for you
        in our middle age

after repeated requests
with the others almost grown
one winter day and your father in
sleepy   attendance in one of the
office rooms downstairs   and everyone else
waiting in the hall   you were finally born

Some Nearly Songs

The Old Dog's Song

Where can I shit
          said the old dog
turning this way and that
the grasses are gone
          the asphalt is slimy with oil
on the nice rubbly lots
          there are six story buildings
where can I shit
          said the old dog
          turning this way and that

Where can I turn
          said the old dog
no one is in heat
          on this block at least
my old friends have altered
   or snap   they show me their teeth
          not their ass
          said the old dog
turning this way and that

This leash is so loose
          said the old dog
turning this way and that
nobody cares if I run
          the children have gone
the man who hangs on is like me
he looks up the block and then down
          turning this way and that
said the old dog
          turning this way and that

34th Street Song

With joy she showed the traveller Macy's
That's Macy's there   right by Korvette's
                    and Gimbels

Oh you were right not to get out at 14th Street
Macy's is nice   but Klein's was the store
                    and it ended

The Sad Children's Song

This house is a wreck said the children
when they came home with their children
Your papers are all over the place
The chairs are covered with books
and look   brown leaves are piled on the floor
under the wandering Jews

Your face is a wreck said the children
when they came home with their children
There are lines all over your face
your necks like curious turtles
Why did you let yourself go?
Where are you going without us?

This world is a wreck said the children
When they came home with their children
There are bombs all over the place
There's no water   the fields are all poisoned
Why did you leave things like this
Where can we go said the children
what can we say to our children?

Traveler

He travels three hundred miles to New York
carrying all the works of Kawabata
when he returns he brings them back with him

What are they doing in his suitcase all that time

Speaking to one another as the books of any author will do
arguing the past and future of technical authority
ghosts invented for melody's sake   It's the tune
the time sings   all our stories are set to it

Sitting in the bus   watching New England curl
around its rivers   thinking of his own long
difficult novel   he will place THE SOUND
OF THE MOUNTAIN on his lap   he will ask
its intelligent advice

Standing in high grass at home imagining farm
  and granary he looks east
      he praises Him
      astonished
and last night as we returned from our long walk
across Luquillo Beach we saw the colorless sun fall
between dark rain and the flashing sea
          I think he praised Him
white birds flew up against the night
But for everyday life, he shows no gratitude

Still his courage is greater than mine
Days pass no voice answers his
        My dear I say
this is because the times are bad
speaker and speaker do not know one another
and the song sung by the people to the singer
is not known
      though the melody is theirs

Quarrel

Bob and I
        in different rooms
        talking to ourselves
carrying on
        last night's
        hard conversation
convinced
        the other one
        the life companion
        wasn't listening

Autumn

1

What is sometimes called a
   tongue of flame
or an arm extended burning
   is only the long
red and orange branch of
   a green maple
in early September   reaching
   into the greenest field
out of the green woods   at the
   edge of which the birch trees
appear a little tattered   tired
   of sustaining delicacy
all through the hot summer re-
   minding everyone (in
our family)   of a Russian
   song   a story
by Chekov   or my father

2

What is sometimes called a
   tongue of flame
or an arm extended   burning
   is only the long
red and orange branch of
   a green maple
in early September   reaching
   into the greenest field
out of the green woods   at the

edge of which the birch trees
appear a little tattered   tired
    of sustaining delicacy
all through the hot summer   re-
    minding everyone   (in
our family)   of a Russian
    song   a story by
Chekov or my father on
    his own lawn   standing
beside his own wood in
    the United States of
America   saying (in Russian)
    this birch is a lovely
tree   but among the others
    somehow superficial

South Window

Man   peeing
         by the woodpile
in the rain
         sky blue   birdblue
poncho

my man
         sometimes
more often
         his own

Man walking into
         deep woods
dark green leaves
         splashing
blue plastic

summer mist
         on hot earth
breathing him
         away

My Father at 85

My father said
            how will they get out of it
            they're sorry they got in

My father says
            how will they get out
            Nixon Johnson   the whole bunch
            they don't know how

goddamit he says
            I'd give anything to see it
            they went in over their heads

he says
            greed   greed   time
            nothing is happening fast enough

My Father at 89

His brain simplified itself
saddening everyone   but he
asked us   children
don't you remember my dog Mars
who met me on the road
when I came home   lonesome
and singing   walking
from the Czar's prison

One Day I Decided

One day I decided to not grow any older
lots of luck I said to myself
(my joking self)   then I looked up at the sky
which is wide   its blueness   its whiteness

low on my left   the steamy sun rose   moved

I placed my hand against it   my whole hand
which is broad from pinky to thumb   no   my
two hands   I bared my teeth to it   my teeth
are strong   secure on their gold posts   I breathed
deeply   I held my breath   I stood on my toes   ah

then I was taller   still the clouds sailed
through me   around me   it's true   I'm just
like them   summertime water that the sun
sips and spits   into this guzzling earth

In Aix

The doves   the speckled doves
are cooing in French   in high
female French   the shutters
clatter against their latches

The rain is the rain of Aix a-
wash in old paintings of
marsh and mist by Granet the rain
splashes the shutters the rain is

bathed in the clouds of Chernobyl
last night on the evening
news we heard how nightingales
blowing north from Poland
folded their wings   fell over
the border and died in Germany

On the Ramblas
      A Tree   A Girl

Anyone would love to paint from memory
the bark of a plane tree in Barcelona
little geographies of burgundy turn to olive
before your very eyes or peel to that yellow
that pale cream of all the apartment rooms
in The Bronx

or write one proper grieving song for the girl
beautiful but burned in face and arm
smoke smeared into lifelong recognition
screaming in Catalan at the man who stands
before her   who supplicates   whose hands
brought together in supplication
beg   for what
        pimp   lover   father?

I say   father   because I'm old
and know how we beg the young to live
no matter what

Oh the dreamer said
and dreamed himself she

it was an unusual day
when all the suns stood
visible and we could see
our light small sighted sun

its rays were bones
of the old wars

In France

Poor talker   mouthperson
    alone
waiting for bravery

the muse (in
    other words)
        OH language

circumvent my tongue
    tell pen
        Move!

Make text

I Gave Away That Kid

I gave away that kidlike he was an old button
    Here old button get off of me
    I don't need you anymore
    go on get out of here
    get into the army
    sew yourself onto the colonel's shirt
    or the captain's fly   jackass
    don't you have any sense
    don't you read the papers
    why are you leaving now?

That kid walked out of here like he was the cat's pyjamas
    what are you wearing p j's for   you damn fool?
    why are you crying   you couldn't
    get another job anywhere anyways
    go march to the army's drummer
    be a man like all your dead uncles
    then think of something else to do

Lost him, sorry about that the president said
    he was a good boy
    never see one like him again
    Why don't you repeat that your honor
    why don't you sizzle up the meaning
    of that sentence for your breakfast
    why don't you stick him in a prayer
    and count to ten before my wife gets you.

That boy is a puddle in Beirut   the paper says
    scraped up for singing in church
    too bad   too bad is a terrible tune
    it's no song at all   how come you sing it?

I gave away that kidlike he was an old button
        Here old button get off ame
        I don't need you anymore
        go on get out of here
        get into the army
        sew yourself onto the colonel's shirt
        or the captain's fly   jackass
        don't you have any sense
        don't you read the papers
        why are you leaving now?

On the Subway Station

The child is speaking to the father
he is looking into the father's eyes
father doesn't answer
child is speaking Vietnamese
father doesn't answer
child is speaking English
father doesn't answer
The father is staring at a mosaic in blue and green
and lavender   three small ships in harbor
set again and again in the white tiled
beautiful   old   unrenovated subway
station   Clark Street   Brooklyn

Bridges

Along the beach beyond La Boca   the Luquillo River
stretches and bends to reach the sea   in tropical
easiness it takes no trouble   at high tide the ad-
venturous sea pours salt into the eyes of the
sweet water fish

Clouds blow and darken toward the mists of the
rain forest mountain   sun falls from the aging
day and looks at night   but first it shines the
palm leaves blinding the lizards

Fifty feet toward sunset the river widens   it was
once two rivers   I can see the far glint of a steel
bridge   cars moving fast on Route Three

A dark form stands in the Luquillo River   an old bridge
pillar and planks rotted   unconnected to either shore

Long ago in morning shadow this bridge rattled the
campesinos and the pescadores in their carts hurrying
to Fajardo   they travelled in sight of the fishy
noisy sea

There were four bridges over the river near Nien Trach
south south of Tonkin Bay   north of Quangh Binh   three
were splintered and burned   torn from their village
shores   one stood   a dyke of mud and rocks as wide
as a small truck

We drive to the airport near San Juan   the sea on one hand
the darkening river   the old unconnected bridge   a platform
on mossy stilts   the traffic is heavy on Route Three
called by American Army Engineers   The Road of the
Sixty-fifth Infantry

103

In Hanoi   1969

Sometimes
on this green hill
I walk around all day
in my cotton shirt and shiny black pajama pants
the rubber tire sandals
that I bought in the Foreigners' Store

The tailor was tired of pleasing Russians
he looked Tuan in the eye and said   an American?
What is the Fatherland Front thinking of now?
there is no cotton   there is very little cotton

He measured carefully   Linda and I were ashamed
to be American and fat   the Russian woman laughed at us
she watched   the tailor said   choose your material   there
are the bolts of cloth   he was disgusted
he said   take anything   what is it worth   this
is the Foreigners' Store   Tuan told us later
he suffers   he is an intelligent man

Then I spoke Russian   the language
my childhood had casually stored   Tell me madame
I don't sew   which is the proper material?

She answered   My dear   that is beautiful   and that too
is good   but that!   only the Vietnamese
would wear   she was nicely dressed
a diplomat's wife   she will travel   she
will buy lovely saris in Delhi   and in North Africa
a djellaba of fine wool   a proud and visiting life
is before her   she will be with her husband an empire's
interested emissary to the quiet edge
of the terrible wars

104

Two Villages

In Duc Ninh a village of 1,654 households
Over 100 tons of rice and casava were burned
18,138 cubic meters of dyke were destroyed
There were 1077 air attacks
There is a bomb crater that measures 150 feet across
It is 50 feet deep

Mr. Tat said: The land is more exhausted than the people
                  I mean to say that the poor earth
                  is tossed about
                  thrown into the air again and again
                  it knows no rest

                  whereas the people have dug tunnels
                  and trenches   they are able in this way
                  to lead normal family lives

In Trung Trach
a village of 850 households
a chart is hung in the House of Tradition

rockets	522
attacks	1201
big bombs	6998
napalm	1383
time bombs	267
shells	12291
pellet bombs	2213

Mr. Tuong of the Fatherland Front
has a little book
in it he keeps the facts
carefully added

105

That Country

This is about the women of that country
sometimes they spoke in slogans
They said
    We patch the roads as we patch our sweetheart's trousers
    The heart will stop but not the transport
They said
    We have ensured production even near bomb craters
    Children let your voices sing higher than the explosions
                        of the bombs
They said
    We have important tasks to teach the children
    that the people are the collective masters
    to bear hardship
    to instill love in the family
    to guide for good health of the children (they must
    wear clothing according to climate)
They said
    once men beat their wives
    now they may not
    once a poor family sold its daughter to a rich old man
    now the young may love one another
They said
    once we planted our rice any old way
    now we plant the young shoots in straight rows
    so the imperialist pilot can see how steady our
    hands are

In the evening we walked along the shores of the Lake
                        of the Restored Sword

I said   is it true?   we are sisters?
They said, Yes, we are of one family

Street Corner Dialogue

Thank God for the old Jewish ladies
    though their sons are splendid with houses
    and brilliant from college
    they take our leaflets

Sometimes they say
    pishers   what's on your mind
    don't get excited   Hitler is
    dead   where are the sweatshops

Then we say   Missus
    did you forget Vietnam
    I won't speak about Israel   turn
    around maybe 80$^{o\pm}$ you'll see a few
    sweatshops   not to mention
    imperialism's furnace   the nation
    of Africa

They answer   of course
    oh yes   as usual   we heard it
    before   naturally ai   the poor
    people are dying   dying   dying
    foolish girl   listen   you'll never
    stop it   the dying from killing

Then we tell them only five words
    So   why did you live?

Uh Oh   a fresh mouth   but
    darling you're right   in your life
    you shouldn't give up the ship   so long
    you got strength   maybe this world
    wouldn't turn out a total disaster

Illegal Aliens

The Chicago Airport
O'Hare
4:30 A.M.

fifty men
in double lines
handcuffed

dark men

probably Mexicans
wearing
the work clothes

in which they were taken

brightness of the airport
the empty shopping stalls blaze

a tall sandy-haired man
leads them   not in uniform
gray pants   an ordinary
windbreaker   he calls
aquí aquí   waving his hands

a young woman in the rear
shouts   go on now
aquí aquí you got to
go the way he says

In San Salvador (I)

Come   look   they said
here are the photograph albums
these are our children

We are called The Mothers of the Disappeared
we are also the mothers of those who were seen once more
and then photographed   sometimes parts of them
could not be found

a breast   an eye   an arm is missing
sometimes a whole stomach
that is why we are called   The Mothers
of the Disappeared   although we have these large
heavy photograph albums full of beautiful
torn faces

In San Salvador (II)

Then one woman spoke   About my son
she said   I want to tell you   This
is what happened

        I heard a cry   Mother
mother   keep the door closed   a scream
the high voice of my son   his scream
jumped into my belly   his voice
boiled there and boiled until hot water
ran down my thigh

        The following week I waited
by the fire making tortilla   I heard What?
the voice of my second son   Mother quickly
turn your back to the door   turn your back
to the window

        And one day of the third week
my third son called me   oh mother please
hurry up   hold out your apron   they are
stealing my eyes

        And then in the fourth week   my
fourth son   No

    No   It was morning   he stood
in the doorway   he was taken right
there   before my eyes the parts of
the body of my son were tormented   are
you listening?   do you understand
this story?   there was only one
child   one boy   like Mary   I had
only one son

110

For Mike and Jeannie: Resisters
Fifteen Years Later

The car turned over three times
rolled down the nice
summertime hayfield

at the riverbank   the boy
hung upside down in his seat belt
glass   glittering dust
          in his hair   on his long lashes
          gently we brushed his bloody lips
          Did I live?   he asked

Then Mike said   Look!   sometimes
          what you see   you see your own death

I want to know
who saw you Mike   with Jeannie
on that Virginia road   six months later
          tilting   tilting into the
          rain softened shoulder   over
          over   down   flung
from that tin can of a car

did one of you see the   other
dead   did one of you say
No   No   Us?

Learning From Barbara Deming

First: She's a listener.
So you can learn something about paying attention.

Second: She's stubborn.
So you can learn how to stand, look into the other's
    face and not run.

Third: She's just.
So you can learn something about patience.

Fourth: She loves us—women I mean—and speaks to
    the world.
So you can learn how to love women and men.

If you have acquired a taste for happiness
                  it's very hard to do without
so you try jollity for awhile
jokes
      and
            merriment

Song is one of the famous methods
for continuing or entrenching
                              happiness

Here is another example of ordinary joy:
            the gathering together of comrades
            in disagreement and resolution
            followed by determined action

Still   the face of life will change
partly because of those miserable scratches it makes
on its own aging surface
                  Then
                  happiness

in the risky busy labor of Repair the World
after which   for the unsated   there will surely be
talking all night   dances in schoolrooms and kitchens
                  and sometimes
                  love
of happinesses   the most famous of all

Definition

My dissent is cheer
a thankless disposition
first as the morning star
    my ambition: good luck

and why not   a flight
over the wide dilemma
and then good night to
    sad forever

Age

Frightened   fearful   afraid
        older   waking in fear
healthy   feet O.K.   appetite
        only teeth half gone   wrists
strong   night love   waking in
        fear   older   old   nothing
ahead   glad to say ah!
        willing   working   tired
laugh!   dance after supper
        knees useful   love   waking
afraid   bad news   friends old
        sickness   becoming well
an occupation a
        hope against age   fear

Love

Handsome men wearing red ties walk past my window
not one but three   this morning!   their coats open
their ties flying   as though spring had made some
deliberate move on our street   maybe a fur-tipped
bud among the hedges   a fact: years and
years ago I saw you pass   your face rosy from that
interior lifelong commotion   your head forward
stubborn against a March wind   day after day
for nearly a month   as you walked with con-
siderable eagerness toward your daily life
right past my window   I thought   who
is that man   then I thought oh
I already know him

Now time himself   the master streamer
grew
by pools and ponds
then strenuously   to accommodate the generations
became a sea

In which the fish and thee
my love   by dark and night light swim
and nations drown

The Women's Prison: El Salvador
The Ballad of Visiting Day

In Ilopongo Prison
        a girl is sitting quietly
She has only one leg   she
        wears a pretty dress and

her hair is done in braids
        her mother sits beside her
wearing a black dress her brother
        whistles through two reeds

and watches the sad women
        In Ilopongo prison
a little prisoner calls out Maria
        come talk to the North Americans

This prisoner has been a woman
        only a short time   she
wears a black beret   she wears
        a sash   she is a commandante

she fought away from girlhood
        in the high mountains of her country
Come come and tell your story
        to the North American women

about your brother Jaime
        martyred while still
a schoolboy   the mother hears
        his name Jaime   Jaime called

out loud   with her hand she brushes
        the dress all full of flowers
that she brought her daughter with one leg

she sighs   she sighs deeply
you would think her body was
        a drum of thumping air

I stood inside our garden
        where we planted beans
the beans were climbing high
        five men came and whispered

—oh we are Jaime's friends
        oh how we long to see him
we knew him in the hills
        the little bumpy hills

that stumbled into mountains
        he said he had a sister
just like a morning rose
        that's how we recognized you

Tell us Maria   rosy beauty
        where is your brother Jaime
he's our brother too
        our comrade

I don't know where he is
        Come now little sister
you must tell us we lack
        all happiness without him

(There were five men)   believe me
        the last time that I saw him
those were the days of rain
        You stupid girl   you're lying

119

You're lying   liar tell us   we'll burn
        your mother's house   we are
the Guard now tell us   then
        one man raised his rifle   why?
I cried out   why?   Lightning
        slapped the earth beside me

All round the prison floor
        the little babies crawled
the mother looked at them
        she smoothed her daughter's dress

(the dress so full of flowers)
        Thank Mary   blessed virgin
that we were spared such shame
        The little commandante

cried out no shame no shame
        she banged the table hard
no shame   these children are not
        the first whose fathers are unknown

We are the babes of rape
        said the little commandante
our villages were torn our mothers
        violated   our fathers split in two

Still we have named our struggle
        for Farabundo Marti and we are
fierce and restless till justice and
        the land belong to the poor people

In Ilopongo Prison
    a girl is sitting quietly
she has only one leg   her mother
    sits beside her brushing
her long hair   her brother
    watches   whistles through two reeds
The little commandante talks
    with the North American women
the babies crying crawl toward
    the breasts of their lonesome mothers

The Dance in Jinoteca

In Jinoteca women greeted us
with thousands of flowers   roses
it was hard to tell   the petals
on our faces and arms   falling

Then embraces and the Spanish language
which is a little like a descent of
petals   pink   and orange

Suddenly out of the hallway our
gathering place   AMNLAE   the
Associacion de Mujeres women
came running   seat yourselves dear
guests from the north   we announce
a play a dance   a play   the women
their faces mountain   river Indian
European   Spanish   dark haired
women

     dance   in grey green
fatigues they dance the Contra who
circles the village waiting
for the young teacher   the health worker
(these are the strategies)   the farmer
in the high village walks out into the
morning toward the front which is a
circle of terror

      they dance
the work of women and men   they dance
the plowing of the field   they kneel
to the harrowing with the machetes   they
dance the sowing of seed (which is always

a dance) and the ripening of corn   the
flowers of grain   they dance the harvest
they raise their machetes for
the harvest   the machetes are high
                    but no!

out of the hallway in green and grey
come those who dance the stealth
of the Contra   cruelly they
dance the ambush   the slaughter of
the farmer they are the death dancers
who found the school teacher   they caught
the boy who dancing   brought seeds in
his hat all the way from Matagalpa they
dance the death of the mother the
father   the rape of the daughter   they
dance the child murdered the seeds
spilled and trampled   they dance
sorrow   sorrow

                    they dance the
search for the Contra   and the defeat
they dance a comic dance they make a
joke of the puppetry of the Contra of
Uncle Sam who is the handler of puppets
they dance rage and revenge   they place
the dead child (the real sleeping baby)
on two chairs   which is the bier for
the little actor they dance prayer
bereavement   sorrow   they mourn

Is there applause for such theater?

Silence   then   come let us dance
together   now   you know   the usual
dance of couples Spanish or North
American   let us dance in twos and
threes   let us make little circles let us
dance as though at a festival or in peace-
time together and alone   whirling   stamping
our feet   bowing to one another

                         the children
gather petals from the floor to throw
at our knees   we dance   the children
too banging into us   into each other and
one small boy dances alone pulling
at our skirts   wait   he screams stop!
he tugs at the strap of our camera   stop!
Stop dancing   I'm Carlos   take a picture
of me   No!   Now!   Right now! because
soon   Look!   See Pepe!   even tomorrow
I could be dead like him

                      the music
catches its breath   the music
jumping in the guitar and phonograph holds
still and waits   no no we say   Carlos
not you   we put our fingers on his little
shoulder   we touch his hair   but one of
us is afraid   for god's sakes take his
picture   so we lift him up   we photo-
graph him   we pass him from one to
another   we photograph him again and
again   with each of us   crying or
laughing with him in our arms
we dance

124

People in My Family

In my family
people who were eighty-two were very different
from people who were ninety-two

The eighty-two year old people grew up
      it was 1914
      this is what they knew
      War   World War   War

That's why when they speak to the child
they say
      poor little one. . .

The ninety-two year old people remember
      it was the year 1905
      they went to prison
      they went into exile
      they said   ah   soon

When they speak to the grandchild
they say
      yes   there will be revolution
      then there will be revolution   then
      once more   then the earth itself
      will turn and turn and cry out oh I
      have been made sick

             then you   my little bud
                 must flower and save it

125

In the Bus

Somewhere between Greenfield and Holyoke
snow became rain
and a child passed through me
As a person moves through mist
as the moon moves through
a dense cloud at night
as though I were cloud or mist
a child passed through me

On the highway that lies
across miles of stubble
and tobacco barns our bus speeding
speeding disordered the slanty rain
and a girl with no name naked
wearing the last nakedness of
childhood breathed in me
                    once no
                    two breaths
a sigh   she whispered   Hey you
begin again
                Again?
again   again   you'll see
it's easy   begin again   long ago